What a Modern Catholic Believes About MORAL PROBLEMS

by
Raymond Bosler

The Thomas More Press
Chicago, Illinois

WHAT A MODERN CATHOLIC BELIEVES ABOUT MORAL PROBLEMS

Contents

PREFACE

THE DAYS of the Catholic "answer man" are gone forever. Vatican Council II put him to rest with these words in its "Constitution on the Church in the Modern World": "Let the layman not imagine that his pastors are always such experts that to every problem which arises, however complicated, they can readily give him a concrete solution, or even that such is their mission."

We Catholics no longer imagine revelation to be a collection of precisely formulated truths handed down to be memorized by generation after generation. Revelation is a living, on-going experience of God. As the council's "Constitution on Revelation" explains it: "through this revelation, therefore, the invisible God, out of the abundance of His love speaks to men as friends and lives among them so that he may invite and take them into fellowship with Himself."

Hence belief, or the act of faith, would seem to be not merely the accepting as true what God teaches through the pastors of the Church, but the loving submission and listening to the living God personally revealing himself to the individual through these teachings. Because it is loving, this submission must include a response, which is nothing else than a striving to understand and to carry out in life what was heard. It is this response of all believers which increases and advances the Church's knowledge of revelation and how it applies to right living.

This book is an attempt to carry on such a dialogue on Catholic moral issues. The questions, which are sometimes actually responses, are all authentic. They came to me for comment in a question-and-answer column that appears in United States and Canadian Catholic newspapers (syndicated by Universal Press Syndicate).

CAN THERE BE DIALOGUE
IN THE CHURCH?

Q.   *There was a time when the teaching role of the Church was not questioned by priests, publicly or privately. The Church was considered of divine origin and therefore had the privilege and function to teach what is right and wrong. In our day, Catholic theologians speak and write as though they know more than the Pope and bishops, saying this and that has to be changed and accusing the Pope and bishops of being imprudent and improper. How come?*

A.   Theologians who take issue with the teaching of the Holy Father or with decisions of the Roman Curia or with pastoral letters of the bishops do not question their authority; rather they are honestly trying to protect and strengthen the teaching authority of the Church. They are performing the role, which they consider indispensable in the Church, of asking the questions and supplying the biblical, historical and scientific knowledge the pope and bishops need to clarify and develop their teaching. This is a role that the ordinary Catholic knew nothing about, for he was brought up to believe that pope and bishops were able to speak for God without any help other than that of the Holy Spirit.

Then came Vatican Council II. One of its great surprises, surely, for both Catholic and Protestant - shocking for some, thrilling for others - was the discovery that bishops of what was thought to be a monolithic church disagreed upon some important issues, some of them mat-

ters that once seemed beyond dispute. This, and
many other things that happened during the four
years of the Council, helped us rediscover a
more realistic and human notion of the Church
that had been lost or distorted during the long
years of defense against the challenge of Prot-
estantism.

We rediscovered St. Augustine's notion of a
pilgrim Church in which pastors and faithful
struggle together through trial and error on the
way to truth. We rediscovered the long neglected truth that the Holy Spirit inspires with
his gifts not only the pope and bishops but all
the faithful. We are made aware of the need
pastors have of seeking the advice and co-
operation of the laity and of the need Catholics
have of the experience of other Christians and
the knowledge of science and modern philosophy
for a better understanding of revelation. Pope
Paul marked the great difference with his first
encyclical in which he called for dialogue – dialogue within the Church, between the churches
and with the world.

We have discovered at long last that the notion of the Church that you and I grew up with
was not adequate and was not traditional. A
quick look at history will show how wrong we
were. St. Bernard did not hesitate in a public
writing to give directions to his pope. Dante, in
his Divine Comedy, a book that modern popes
have compared with the Summa of St. Thomas
Aquinas as a model of Catholic thinking, placed
popes of his time in his fictional hell. And a
young girl in her twenties, St. Catherine of
Siena, told her pope he was wrong to remain at

Avignon and talked him into returning to Rome.

The Pope today depends upon theologians to help him write his messages, speeches and encyclicals. He has recently set up an international commission of theologians, some of whom had previously discussed his writings critically. Theologians and other experts including historians, biblical scholars and church lawyers have a duty to publish what they know and to take issue with Church authorities when the advancement of truth and the need of souls is at stake. In this modern age, especially in the Western World where so many laity are well educated, this should be a public dialogue and not done in private correspondence as in the past when uneducated peasants and serfs might have been confused by differences of opinion among their pastors.

I grant you that all this is not easy to live with, particularly since some theologians and priests have not yet learned how to dialogue with pope and bishops with the charity, discretion and respect for authority required for an orderly and successful advancement toward truth. But, be patient and have confidence in the Holy Spirit. Somehow he managed to lead the bishops through the unpleasant disagreements and faith-threatening experiences of the Council. I think he is now leading the whole Church through a similar experience.

WHAT IS SERIOUS SIN?

Q. *How can the institutional Church create sins for the damnation of human souls? How, for example, can she command attendance at mass, even for seven-year-olds "under pain of mortal sin?" And how can she say that eating meat on Ash Wednesday constitutes a serious sin? Pray, sir, if eating a ham sandwich on Ash Wednesday is a serious sin, what are we to make of blasphemy, murder, rape, incest and matters that really move man away from God? Are you content to state merely that they are serious sins too?*

A. No, sir, I am not. I sympathize with your agonizing, and I blame your condition upon the faulty religious instruction you must have received.

A mortal sin is the full, deliberate choosing of some created good as a final end in preference to the Supreme Good which is God. A child of seven is not capable of such a choice. He may know from his religious instruction that to miss mass on Sundays is a serious sin; he may even mistakenly, from faulty instruction, think that he is damned to hell because he missed mass; but surely before God he is not old enough to make the ultimate decision required for mortal sin. A boy of twelve is capable of committing murder, but no jury would give him the same sentence it would give to a grown man.

The gravity of sin is measured by the extent of the disorder and aversion to God caused by the sinful act and its consequences and also by the dispositions of the sinner. When you get right down to it, sin is a failure to love God and fellow men. It is conceivable, therefore, that neglect of Sunday mass could be a greater sin than murder, if the neglect of the Sunday obligation were rooted in contempt for God and the act of murder were the result of maddening anger.

Theologians today are having second thoughts about whether the Church can require the observance of her own laws under the pain of mortal sin. She can and should make laws regulating worship, the administration of the sacraments, the organization of her institutions, etc., and some of these she can declare more serious than others. But it is hard to understand how the breaking of such rules could be serious sins in themselves. If they are serious sins, they are so because they are failures to love under some heading. Thus to miss Sunday mass without reason could be a serious sin because it was an act of contempt for God or a serious scandal to one's children. In both cases love would be offended.

You will notice that what I am doing here is putting more stress on the motives, the circumstances and the relation to love. That is what recent moral theology attempts to do. It does not deny the necessity of law; it does not neglect moral principles; but it opposes the oversimplification of the recent past which described sanctity as keeping laws and sin as breaking them.

Q. *If a person makes a good confession but does not confess some doubtful mortal sins, are the doubtful mortal sins forgiven? Also may a person receive Holy Communion when there is doubt about a mortal sin, especially if he has made an act of contrition?*

A. I shall begin by giving you the answer you want and then add something for which you may not have bargained.

Your problem has to do with two laws of the Church. One is Canon 901 of the Code of Canon Law, which restates a law of the Council of Trent that requires a member of the Church to confess all mortal sins "of which one after earnest examination of conscience knows he is guilty." If after an adequate examination of conscience you honestly doubt whether you freely consented to a sin or were fully aware of what you were doing, then you do not "know" that you sinned seriously and, therefore, you are not obliged to mention it in confession. Even though in reality the sin were serious, it would be forgiven in the confession so long as your sorrow extended to all serious sins you may have committed.

The other law is Canon 856, also based upon regulations of the Council of Trent, which states that "no one who is conscious of having committed mortal sin, even if he believes himself to be contrite, should approach the Holy Eucharist without first making a sacramental confession." If you are in doubt, you are not "conscious of having committed mortal sin"; so you may receive Holy Communion without confession.

So much for the law. But there is something about your attitude to sin that seems too selfish, too lacking in love of God who may have been offended by your sin. I don't blame you. Most of us were brought up to think of sin too much in legal terms and to examine our consciences for individual acts of sin that might need forgiving rather than our general attitude toward God.

Some recent spiritual writers urge us to look upon sin less as isolated acts than a basic orientation of the personality away from God's friendship. They look upon the moral law as an invitation from God to develop an open personality, one related affectively to other persons – divine and human. Sin is considered a refusal of that invitation.

That refusal may be expressed in one action, but normally a serious sin is an action that has been prepared for gradually by the adoption of an indifferent attitude toward God and fellowmen. Examinations of conscience, these writers suggest, should center on one's basic attitude and orientation.

If our basic attitude toward God is a willingness to cooperate in carrying out God's plan for ourselves and for others, then the presumption in a doubtful situation is that we have not sinned.

If a husband seriously injures or temporarily terminates his love relationship with his wife, he surely knows it. The same should be true of our relationship with God.

A serious violation of the love relationship between husband and wife, like adultery, has usually been prepared for by numerous "little" infidelities through which a basic attitude has been formed. The same would seem to be true of man's relationship with God.

If, however, we look at sin only as an act that violates a law, we tend to separate it from our basic attitude toward God. Then when we go to confession we are concerned with erasing the guilt of the act more than with our personal relationship with God. It is this relationship that needs to be examined and improved through the Sacrament of Penance. Our anxiety can then center on the dispositions and attitudes that injure that relationship, and the question of whether or not we sinned seriously in one particular act takes on importance primarily in so far as it reveals a faulty attitude in our personal relationship with God.

Concern with the overall relationship rather than individual acts diminishes the intensity of the search for security in one's relationship with God, and this is healthy. Today we need fewer security seekers and more spiritual adventurers. The commitment of faith seems to lose something if it does not have a leap-in-the-dark character.

HOW ABOUT SUNDAY MASS?

Q. *How about some light on the obligation of Sunday mass? Many elderly people risk life and limb to go to mass on abominable icy days and even in blizzards, when anybody but an acrobat would be wiser to stay home. But some young people seem to have the idea since Vatican II that they are free to skip mass just because they don't feel like going to Church or it "isn't a meaningful experience." How anything can be a meaningful experience if one refuses to experience it, I cannot imagine.*

A. The youngsters, I think are revolting against the rigoristic interpretation of the law of Sunday observance taught to the oldtimers. It was the oversimplified teaching that to miss mass was a mortal sin which frightened older Catholics into thinking they must risk their limbs to attend mass and even confess as sinful masses missed through no fault of their own.

The younger generation no longer considers credible the assertion that God would punish with eternal damnation a man who missed mass on Sunday without a reason. It's time theologians and canonists help them and the oldtimers understand what the Sunday mass obligation is all about.

Church law does impose attendance at mass on Sundays and certain holy days as a serious obligation. It could be a mortal sin to flagrantly disobey it. But this is a law not to be interpreted with a Germanic or Anglo-Saxon approach to law, but with a Roman attitude.

Roman laws are written overly strict on the assumption that dispensations from them will be granted and individuals may readily find excuses for judging they do not apply in given circumstances. In Latin countries, accordingly, where Roman law tradition prevails, the Sunday observance has rested rather lightly upon the the populace.

The Latins readily find excuses for missing mass. The good Catholics among them are very faithful about Sunday mass and even weekday mass. Rarely, however, among these would there be anyone who would judge himself guilty of serious sin for missing mass. There is a lesson here.

In the Latin countries those who attend mass faithfully do so not because they feel obliged under pain of mortal sin, but because they feel that this is what a good, sincere Catholic does. And this, it seems to me, is the idea we must plant in the minds of our young.

Q. *Can one make a bad Confession without knowing he is doing so?*

Is it a sin to be distracted while praying, and if so, must this be confessed?

I must take my three small children to mass with me each Sunday. They are a distraction and many times I find I cannot fully concentrate on what's going on, even during the principal parts of the mass. I worry sometimes whether or not I am fulfilling my obligation. Yet I cannot attend mass without bringing my children with me.

A. Questions like these are asked all the time. They reflect more fear than love of God, and I suspect they result from early religious training which stressed letter-perfect service to a stern all-knowing God. In an effort to inculcate discipline and obedience too many teaching Sisters – and priests, too – in the past forgot to stress equally hard the everlasting compassion and mercy of a God all too aware of human frailty.

Somehow we must get across to children, particularly, that it is a generous love of God, expressed through the duties of faith, that is pleasing. Not any specific set of duties in themselves. And that those who act out of love and do the best they can are going to please him.

We have a duty to know and cherish the tenets of our faith, to practice with devotion those obligations which mark us as Catholics, but we must guard against a scrupulousness which is concerned only with the details of the law and not the spirit of love from which they grew.

We cannot sin without knowledge or make a "bad" confession without being aware of it. We cannot sin without intent. Distractions while praying are not the exclusive province of ordinary men. The saints had their problems in this matter, too. Most people would acknowledge that any mother who undertakes the work of readying three small children for church so that she may fulfill her obligation to attend mass, has already proved her devotion to the law.

Q. *Help me to return to Sunday mass. I am a*

teenager and the mass turns me off. Even the guitar mass bores me. My grandfather actually loves to go to mass. He goes everyday. He can't understand my attitude. Is this a generation gap? I'd give anything to love to go to mass, but I don't. The way I feel I think it's better to stay away.

A. I feel the same way about playing a piano. I envy those who can ripple the keys with great abandon and amuse themselves and others seemingly without any effort. I can't play at all because I hated to practice and gave up after a few lessons.

All the arts, all the fine achievements of life require effort. Prayer, both private and public, is an art. We don't learn to pray naturally and without effort any more than we learn to play the piano well or paint a beautiful picture without effort. Learning to pray is a challenge to us and learning to pray the mass, the highest form of prayer, is the greatest challenge of all. Don't give up because you find it hard.

There are probably other things that turn you off but which you keep at because you know they are important for your future success and happiness – like school.

I have no quarrel to pick with those who want to make the mass more meaningful and attractive for teenagers, but I do take issue with those who leave them under the impression that mass should always be a joyful and exciting experience and that when one is not in the mood for celebrating it might be better to worship God under the trees or by visiting the sick.

There is a time for finding God under the trees and in the sick, but there is also a time for joining with others in worshipping God in the highest form of prayer. This can be a most rewarding and satisfying experience, but like any art, particularly when performed with others, it demands discipline and much practice before it comes easily.

I have an idea that the reason why many adults who were satisfied with the old mass are unhappy with the new is because we pastors have not asked them to discipline themselves enough by learning to sing and respond in the new liturgy. Priests and people have not worked hard enough at the new liturgy to do it with ease and therefore with satisfaction.

WHAT ABOUT CONFESSION?

Q. *I feel the need of going to confession, but I am all confused. The last time I went - a long, long time ago - the priest said to me: "I don't want you to go to confession like this any more; get with it and modernize your method." What's the new way?*

Q. *Is it true that a person at age 75 doesn't have to go to confession? What have old people got to confess?*

Q. *How should a person address the confessor? Our pastor doesn't want us to say "Bless me, Father." He doesn't want us to enumerate our venial sins. What do we do?*

A. I could fill this book with questions concerning difficulties with confession. Let's try to bring a few basic questions together and deal with them.

Catholics are bound by law to confess once a year all mortal sins committed since their last confession, mentioning the kind and number of these sins. This obligation is usually attached to the "Easter duty" since forgiveness of mortal sins would be necessary in order to receive Holy Communion. However, if a person has no mortal sins to confess he is not bound by law to go to confession at any time. He would not have to go to confession after 35 or 75 or whatever, if he were not aware of seriously offending God.

Church law, in its present form, is concerned with basic minimum requirements considered necessary for the welfare of Catholics. The conscientious Catholic, however, will look to the Gospel as well as to ecclesiastical law for his guidelines and so will not be content with the minimum. He will be concerned with the spirit of Christ's message as well as with the letter of Church law.

This means that he will see confession not as an isolated act that he feels compelled to perform every week, or every month, or before every first Friday, but rather as an important and meaningful part of his whole Christian life. He will recall that the sacraments exist for man and not man for the sacraments, and so he will use the Sacrament of Penance when he feels it will help him, that is, when he recognizes the need to improve his attitudes and behavior in specific ways and is ready to do just that.

Confession, to him, will not be a means of gaining points with a calculating God, but rather a loving reconciliation with Christ and the Church after he has decided to change those aspects of his life which would tend to break or weaken the ties which unite him to God and his fellow men.

So, in preparing for confession, he does not merely recall the list of "sins" which he always mentions, but instead, he takes a good sincere look at the direction of his life to see where he might have slipped away from his ideal of love and service of God and neighbor. Perhaps he will discover serious offenses. These must be mentioned in confession. More likely, he will simply uncover certain smaller aspects of his attitudes and behavior that need to be improved upon if he is to be the kind of Christian he wants to be. Some or all of these may be mentioned according to the penitent's intention to do something about them. Whether he does this according to a set formula ("Bless me, Father . . . etc.") or in a more informal, perhaps conversational way, is up to him and to his confessor.

This, I take it, is what confessors mean when they speak of a "modern" or "adult" way of going to confession. They don't want to listen to a "grocery list" of venial sins repeated over again time after time. They want some assurance that the penitent has taken a look at his situation in life, his obligations to family and society and comes with serious plans to become a better witness to Christ. That is why they like for the penitent to identify himself, not by name but by occupation, state in life, as father, teacher, lawyer, etc.

This way of approaching the Sacrament of Penance presupposes a grasp of Christian morality which is sound and well-informed. How often does a confessor hear a penitent say, "I missed mass because I was sick" or "I neglected my morning prayers" or "I let my teeth touch the host"? Quite often, I suspect. These statements are symptoms of a faulty approach to Christian morality.

It may well be that a good deal of confusion and anxiety surrounding the Sacrament of Penance today could be cleared up if the priests who are dissatisfied with their people's confessions would devote some time to instructing them in depth on the whole area of Christian morality rather than simply telling them to go to confession differently. Now that confession lines are shorter and people are confessing less often, there is opportunity for more instruction in the confessional.

Q. *I find many of the questions you answer idiotic, and I wonder why you answer them. For example: the one about confession: "Is it true that a person at age 75 doesn't have to go to confession? What have old people got to confess?" You were evasive; you didn't give the hard facts.*

I am not 75, but I could be included in the "old people" category. I and others old can commit the following sins: 1) murder; 2) exploit the poor; 3) spew out and teach others hate, venom and malice for individuals and groups because they are black, white, yellow, Irish, Italian, Communist, Catholic, Protestant, Jew, Moslem, etc.; 4) destroy the reputation of others by lies, confidential information, etc. The list could go on indefinitely.

A. I bow to the wisdom of old age.

Q. *I need help, I have had an "affair" and have not been to confession since or during. I am so guilt-ridden I can't forgive me, how could a priest? How could God? I have practically despaired of heaven. And I don't hate the fellow involved. I enjoyed it. Why don't I hate him? What should I do? Do you think God has forgiven*

*me? How can I get the emotional courage to tell
a priest? If he starts talking about it to me, I
know I'll crack up.*

A. Of course God has forgiven you. And you
are closer to him than before, because you recognize your need of him. How can you know God
has forgiven you? The very fact that you are
aware that you have done something wrong is a
grace of God. The very fact that you feel that
you could not "forgive me" indicates that God
has helped you recognize how wrong you were.
There is nothing unusual about the fact that you
do not hate the fellow and that you "enjoyed"
the experience. You now have an insight into
just what sin is and how it happens. Sin is the
giving in to the attraction of a good that we
chose in place of the Supreme Good that is God.
That attraction is always with us. You now have
a better realization of this and should more
humbly recognize how totally you depend upon
God's help to overcome the attraction in the
future. You should also realize now how important it is to read about the goodness of God,
especially in the Scriptures, and to pray so that
you have personal experience of the closeness
of that goodness.

All that you need do now is go and admit to
the Church that you failed as a Christian. This
you can do in the privacy of the confessional.
Is this asking so much in return for the mercy
God has shown you? Don't make it harder than
it is. Tell the priest simply: "I have had an affair; I have broken it off, and now I want to
start my life over." Let him carry on from
there.

AND THE PROBLEMS OF SEX?

Q. *I am 53 years old and a mother of five. All my life I have been troubled with impure thoughts, which cause me great distress because I feel responsible for my thinking. In the last two years my mind has become really sick, as the thoughts are crazy, mixed up with Jesus and sex. My confessor says let them come, and I go to communion every time I go to mass. Should I keep going to Communion? How can I make myself feel I'm not to blame?*

A. I suspect that along with a great number of adults of your generation you are the victim of a faulty education in sex. You were probably taught to look upon all sexual thoughts as impure thoughts and as something displeasing to God. That's what the old prayer-book examinations of conscience tended to do for us, wasn't it? "Took pleasure in impure thoughts . . . . was guilty of immodest actions."

This was misleading. Sexual thoughts are not impure; sexual actions are not immodest, unless they are misdirected. There was a tendency in the approach to identify the prohibited unchaste thought or action with the physical phenomenon of the reproductive drive. The sex drive was presented as something dangerous, nasty, impure, that somehow mysteriously became all right once a marriage ceremony was gone through. No thought whatsoever was given to preparing the young to enjoy and appreciate in marriage the sexual aspect of love.

If you were brought up in such an atmosphere, it is not surprising that you have had problems. A mother of five without sexual thoughts would be a being from outer space. Take your confessor's advice and ignore the thoughts that bother you.

Q. *Is masturbation a mortal sin? And may I add I am no teenager?*

A. In many manuals of moral theology, masturbation is listed under "unnatural sins of impurity" and is described as "complete sexual satisfaction obtained by some source of self stimulation" (*Jonet Moral Theology No. 228*). The manuals go on to say that willful masturbation is always a serious sin. However, if it happens unintentionally and therefore is not a willful, free act, the authors say there is no sin involved. Some would qualify this by adding that, even if such an act occurs unintentionally, one must remain passive and not consent to it.

Theologians today are taking a new look at the problem of masturbation in the light of new knowledge of psychology and sex. Some experts feel that while the teaching of the manuals is correct, it does not give enough attention to the many influences which reduce or remove one's freedom in performing this act, and, therefore, reduce the sinfulness involved. They point out that while a person may knowingly and, in a sense, willingly masturbate, this action may be brought on by any number of physical and/or psychological pressures which reduce the freedom of choice which is necessary for serious sin. They cite studies in which it is shown that many instances of masturbation occur when the person is tense, depressed, or extremely tired. These pressures, they say, can and frequently do limit the freedom of the act, and so not every act of masturbation, even when performed consciously, would be seriously sinful.

Others point out that the practice of masturbation is the rule, rather than the exception, among adolescents and that often the youth confessing masturbation has not broken off his relationship of love with God and neighbor, which is, after all, what serious sin is all about.

As a practical suggestion, I recommend that a person confronted with the problem of masturbation look into his heart as honestly as he can and try to discover the reasons for his acts. If he finds that masturbation is one symptom of a generally self-centered life and that, in many other ways as well, he consistently tends to prefer his own well-being and pleasure to the demands of God and neighbor, then he may well be concerned about his moral situation.

If, on the other hand, he discovers that his occasional acts of masturbation, which he may consider morally wrong in themselves, are out of character with the rest of his life and that they do not change his general relationship of love and concern for God and neighbor, then he may conclude that the individual acts are not seriously sinful and may look upon them as reminders that he is a sinful human in constant need of God's help to overcome sinful tendencies.

This same rule of thumb may be applied by those who from a long habit fall more frequently. Some of these are compulsive masturbators who need psychiatric help.

Q. *What is the Church's attitude toward homosexuality? I don't mean to be hostile or uncharitable, but is it sinful to avoid such people?*

A. It would be sensible not sinful to avoid such people if they were an occasion of sin for you. But most normal people are in no danger.

Surely the Christian thing to do in the case of this sin, as in all others, is to condemn the sin but pity the sinner. Homosexuals need help and understanding.

One of the main reasons why they find it difficult to overcome their unfortunate tendency to be immorally attracted to members of their own sex is because society has made homosexuals seem, in their own minds at least, to be outcasts and unwanted. They feel, therefore, that their situation is hopeless and decide that only another of their own kind can ever befriend them.

Doctors who work with them to overcome their illness - and they are ill - encourage them to become active in projects and organizations, to "get out of themselves" and sublimate their tendencies in good causes. You can, as you see, help the homosexual to conquer his or her problem by encouraging them to take part in worthwhile activities with you or by inviting them to parties where they can be with many people.

The teaching Church has said very little about the problem of homosexuality. The theologians of the Church quite generally agree that homosexuals should be impressed with the fact that God tempts no one beyond his strength, that they like anyone else tempted to the misuse of sex can count on the grace of God to win out over their evil inclinations in the end. But today, theologians are aware that grace will not cure all physical defects, that homosexuality is primarily a problem for the psychiatrist whose help must be enlisted so that grace can build upon nature.

Q. As a Catholic homosexual, I am especially grateful for your response to the question on how to treat homosexuals. No one but a homosexual can know the horror of being "outcast" and "unwanted," the fear of exposure to family, friends, employers; the constant threat of blackmail; the knowledge that never can he know the happiness and security of a home and family of his own; the realization that, as he grows older, there is nothing but loneliness and growing resentment. Resentment, because no one who is homosexual asked to be this way, chose to be this way; resentment of the fact that the society – the family – that produced the neurosis legislates against it, refusing to accept the increasing problem, rejecting its own sons and brothers.

As you note, psychiatry may help in many cases, but not in all; it is not a "cure." After several years and several thousands of dollars of therapy with a prominent psychiatrist, I dis-

covered that the neurosis was so deeply rooted there was no possibility of cure. I was on the verge of suicide until I was fortunate enough to come into contact with an understanding priest. He saved my life, literally, by convincing me that homosexuals can be productive, helpful, good people. And most of the homosexuals I know really are good people; many of us are daily communicants.

A wise theologian wrote me recently that man comes, finally, to God through love of people, and that he achieves love of people because of his love for a person. This has been true in my own case, certainly.

Perhaps the time is past due for the Church and society to evaluate people for what they are as persons, for what they are becoming, not as members of some reviled category or other. Perhaps the time is past due for men, homosexual or not, to cease the self-loathing, the self-destroying sense of guilt, the self-pity, and to begin to live productive lives for the betterment of themselves, their society and the Kingdom of God.

A.   Need anything more be said?

Q.   *Yes more should be said. When our children read about practicing homosexuals being daily communicants, they will be shocked. Since your words look suspiciously like a gesture of approval for what the homosexuals do to and with each other it does call for a reasoned explanation.*

A. An alcoholic can conquer his urges and not get drunk. Daily communion helps him do it. The one still remains an alcoholic; the other still a homosexual.

The homosexual stated that several thousand dollars of therapy from a psychiatrist failed to cure him. He didn't bring this up as justification for giving in to his desires. He merely pointed out that this made it impossible to have the friendship and happiness of married life and made for a lonely existence. And he pointed out that he fortunately had learned that in spite of his affliction he could be a productive and helpful member of society. Everything he said implied that he was mastering his urges and that kindness, understanding and friendship of others were helping him do it.

THE PROBLEMS OF MARRIAGE

Q. *Picture, if you can, a bride-to-be, four to six months pregnant. Friends throw a big bridal shower. Then comes the wedding in church, complete with the bride in flowing white gown and veil, four bridesmaids or more, two flower girls, a ringbearer, a big wedding reception.*
Now I ask you, are the parents, the Church and the community condoning pre-marital sex when it is apparent to all that within a few months after this elaborate celebration the reason for the nuptial makes its premature appearance?

A. Picture, if you can, a nosey busybody probing into affairs that are none of her business. More than likely, no one knew anything about the condition of the bride at the time of the wedding but a few catty parish gossips. But, granting for the sake of argument that it was generally known, why conclude that the Church and community were condoning the sin? Wouldn't it be more charitable to conclude that the Church and community were helping the couple and their families rectify an unfortunate mistake?

Q. *I was brought up to believe that the traditional white gown and veil were symbols of purity and virginity. Has this belief gone out the window? I think we're all getting sick and tired of the too-often-used "be charitable, anybody can make a mistake."*

Q. Your answer both shocks and sustains me. A few years ago my daughter had to marry the boy she was going with. They genuinely loved each other. After my own grief was put aside, I realized they needed all the adult support they could get in order not to go off the deep end, but settle down and establish a new family; one that eventually might become Christian in every sense. I felt that only by putting aside my own moral teachings and feelings could I help in this new venture.

Q. Thanks for your uncharitable reply to what was in fact a very serious question. Within the last two years our parish has had only two weddings that were not "have to" marriages. Statistics say the illegitimate birth rate is rising alarmingly.

If girls knew they would be denied a nice wedding with all the trimmings, would they make that mistake? Shouldn't the church have rules of etiquette in such matters or should it act like an over-indulgent parent?

A. I did not intend to be uncharitable or flippant about such a serious matter. Premarital sex cannot be approved or condoned and I am sorry if I gave that impression.

I was trying to point out the need for understanding and accepting the good intentions of two people who have come to church to be joined together before God. It is not a matter of putting aside moral teachings but of reserving judgment in the face of human frailty.

The white gown, veil and other trimmings of a big church wedding are not matters of morality but of custom. The past sins of the couple are in the province of the confessional, not the society pages. It does seem, however, that the bride's parents – who, after all, bear the financial burden of the elaborate ceremony – could demand that restraint and good taste be exercised, even if the expectant bride has her heart set on "the works."

I agree fully with those who recognize the danger of blandly assuming such circumstances are acceptable. There is, indeed, the risk that other young couples will think such weddings are routine or normal.

Q. *Three years ago my wife had an ovary and tube removed because she had a benign tumor. Last year she gave birth to our fourth child and had her other tube tied. I consented reluctantly. The doctor who performed the operation said it was in the best interest because he found the other ovary was in bad shape. I've been living with this guilt all this time and my conscience has been haunting me. Is it possible to be forgiven so I can have peace of mind again?*

A. It is always possible to be forgiven. If you feel that you made a sinful decision, mention it in confession and start over. Guilty or not in your decision, there is nothing now that forbids your marital relations, if that is what bothers you.

I find the action of your doctor peculiar. If

the ovary was in bad shape, he should have removed it. This he would have been allowed to
do in a Catholic hospital. Maybe you misunder-
stood him and that's what he did and all your
guilt feelings were needless.

Q. *Is intercourse a sin for a married couple
past the child bearing stage?*

A. Of course not.

Q. *I have a personal problem and would appreciate any advice you could give me. My husband
and I have been married for four years. We are
both Catholic and were married in the Church.*

*It has been my ideal in life to raise a family
and to provide a good home life such as my parents gave me. We discussed children many
times before marriage. Right after we were
married, he suggested that, if possible, he
would like to wait a while to have children in
order to "get ahead." I must admit that although
I was not for the idea it did seem to work for a
few months longer.*

*That is where it began. From that time it
was: "Wait until we get a house, a new car,
purchase stocks, etc." The list is endless. We
are financially better off than most people.*

*But it has destroyed my love for him. I find
no happiness in material goods. It has become
a constant source of argument between us. I
have given serious thought to leaving him, as I
feel I am not living in God's grace this way.*

A. You don't need advice; you already know

what's wrong. You both heard the advice of the wedding instruction. "And if true love and the unselfish spirit of perfect sacrifice guide your every action, you can expect the greatest measure of earthly happiness that may be allotted to man in this vale of tears," and promptly ignored it.

In a sense you are to be pitied. You are victims of the current, crazy pattern of living that induces young people to think they must begin married life at the level their parents have reached at the time they leave home. The only hope of saving your marriage that I can see is for you to admit that you were also at fault. More than likely you didn't shed any tears over the new car, the new house, and the expensive furniture and dresses that were doubtless part of that "etc."

You both need to go to a priest or marriage counsellor to hear someone tell you bluntly that you have been just plain selfish.

Q. *I am a Catholic, but very much on the outside. Not having received communion for the last two years, I've lately stopped going to Sunday mass. The reason is birth control.*

We have been married five and a half years and had three children right in a row. The youngest is now two. After each child we truly attempted being faithful to the Church's only permissible methods of abstinence and rhythm. It didn't work. After our last child I went on the pill. What troubles me is that I think I am not doing wrong. I feel for my present children's sake, my own sanity and congeniality with my husband, what we have decided together is for the best.

This is the first time my head has been above water. Our family unity has vastly improved because I'm physically and emotionally up to snuff. What troubles me though is being on the outside with the Church. My education was Catholic from the grades through college. It is an awful feeling to be placed on the outside because I have used my mind for the first time.

I want desperately to receive communion again and make my life eternally rewarding. Two priests have refused me absolution and said until I can obey the rules, I am not a Catholic. Other religions have no meaning for me. Right now I am in no man's land, just drifting. Yet in conscience I can't agree with the papal encyclical. Isn't there any hope for me within the Church?

A. Yes, there is hope for you. You are educated. Why don't you read? Read the whole encyclical *Humanae Vitae*, and read the statements of the United States and Canadian bishops on how to form one's conscience in the light of papal teaching.

The bishops of the United States point out (something obvious from a careful reading of the encyclical) that *Humanae Vitae* does not discuss the question of the good faith of those who make practical decisions in conscience against what the Church considers the divine law and the will of God. "The encyclical," they say, "does not undertake to judge the consciences of individuals, but to set forth the authentic teaching of the Church...."

The U.S. bishops recognize what Pope Paul in the encyclical himself acknowledged, that "married couples faced with conflicting duties are often caught in agonizing crises of conscience," finding it "difficult to harmonize the sexual expression of conjugal love with respect for the life-giving powers of sexual union and the demands of responsible parenthood."

Far from teaching that such persons were cut off from the Church and should be refused the sacraments, Pope Paul urges them to get help from the Eucharist and then says, "And if sin should still keep its hold over them, let them not be discouraged but rather have recourse with humble perseverance to the mercy of God, which is poured forth in the sacrament of penance." This seems to be an admission that circumstances lessen the guilt of those who resort to contraceptives for serious reasons, else he could not have urged perseverance in receiving the sacraments without calling for the determination to give up the practice immediately. This is the interpretation the U.S. bishops give, for they state: "We feel bound to remind Catholic married couples when they are subjected to the pressures which prompt the Holy Father's concern, that however circumstances may reduce moral guilt, no one following the teaching of the Church can deny the objective evil of artificial contraception itself. With pastoral solicitude we urge those who have resorted to artificial contraception never to lose heart but to continue to take full advantage of the strength which comes from the sacrament of penance and the grace, healing and peace in the Eucharist."

The French bishops go further when they say: "Contraception can never be a good. It is always a disorder, but this disorder is not always culpable. It happens, indeed, that spouses see themselves confronted with veritable conflicts of duties . . . . On this subject we shall simply recall the constant teaching of morality, when one has an alternative choice of duties and, whatever may be the decision, evil cannot be avoided, traditional wisdom makes provision for seeking before God which duty in the circumstances is the greater. Husband and wife will decide at the end of a common reflection carried on with all the care that the greatness of their conjugal vocation requires. They can never forget or despise any of the duties in conflict. They will therefore keep their heart disposed to the call of God, attentive to any new possibility that might lead to a revision of their choice or their behavior."

The Canadian bishops put it this way: "In accord with the accepted principles of moral theology, if these persons have tried sincerely but without success to pursue a line of conduct in keeping with the given directives, they may be safely assured that whoever honestly chooses that course which seems right to him does so in good conscience."

You will note that in all this teaching, man does not make up his own morality and decide for himself what is right or wrong. He experiences a crisis precisely because he wants to follow the papal teaching on birth control and yet at the same time fulfill what he knows to be moral obligations to preserve his marriage and raise his children properly. Here is where even one who accepts the direction and teaching of the Church must still make decisions for himself.

You and other Catholics have made such a decision. If you are convinced before God that you are right then you have no sin to confess, though, as the French bishops advise, you must be "disposed to the call of God, attentive to any new possibility that might lead to a revision" of your decision.

Q. *Is it sinful for a married couple to permit a lovemaking climax without the marital act? We do not want any more children, but have never used artificial means of birth control.*

A. This is something that you alone can decide. You are in a difficult situation, for you have decided not to have more children and yet are determined to follow the Church's official teaching against the use of artificial contraceptives. At the same time you must maintain the intimacy of married life and foster love for one another. If your expression of love sometimes leads into something you did not intend, you may decide you were guilty of no sin. If it should happen that you decide from the beginning to procure a climax, you may conclude that you acted sinfully.

Whatever happens, it seems to me that persons such as you, determined to live up to an ideal, are not going to sin seriously if occasionally you fail.

Q. *What is the Church's position on the problem of overpopulation? We are expecting our fifth child and, when reading and hearing constantly about "our crowded earth," we begin to question if it is wise or even responsible to have more children.*

A. The Church has no official position on the problem of overpopulation, but recent popes and Vatican Council II have called attention to moral principles that should be heeded by experts and governments attempting to solve the problem. What these all boil down to is the advice G. K. Chesterton gave a long time ago: when there are more men than hats to go around, try manufacturing more hats before cutting off heads.

The Fathers of Vatican Council II were aware of the seriousness of the overpopulation problem. They recognized the rights and duties of governments with regard to the population problems of their own nation, and they urged Catholic experts to help solve the problem. What is more they went so far as to say: "Human beings should also be judiciously informed of scientific advances in the exploration of methods by which spouses can be helped in arranging the number of their children. The reliability of these methods should be adequately proven and their harmony with the moral order should be clear."

They did, however, make it clear that governments must respect the rights of parents to determine the number of their children. And the danger of government interference in family life is already imminent when lawmakers begin to clamor for regulations limiting families to two children.

Undoubtedly there is a problem of overpopulation – immediately acute in under-developed nations like those in South America and Asia and eventually for the whole world. But so long as we pay farmers for not growing food, we are making fools of ourselves in this under-populated, over-fed, wealthy North America when we have panicked so badly that people like you are tempted to feel they are crowding the earth with five children.

The generation now getting married in this country will not be having large families, and this applies also to Catholics. I can vouch for this from my own parish experience. The day may come when some congressman will clamor for generous tax exemptions to encourage large families.

DIVORCE AND REMARRIAGE

Q. *Is it a sin to occasionally "date" a divorced person? I am a 40-year-old female, have never been married and was raised by strict Catholic parents. The single men in my age group are scarce, and the few that I know do not seem to enjoy the type of entertainment that I do.*

Sometimes a divorced acquaintance will ask me out to dinner or to a special event, but I always turn them down because I've been told it is not allowed by the Church, but, frankly, I'm confused. Why is it wrong? I realize there is the danger of falling in love and marrying outside the Church. But in my mind this is not conceivable. Like other single mature adults, I do not find it easy to fall in love at this stage of life. Also I have passed up many chances of entering a Catholic marriage, and at this point I'm not about to cast aside my religion.

A. In your case I do not think it would be sinful to date a divorced person. You are confused because you mistakenly have concluded that the Church forbids such a date. What the Church forbids is what reason would tell us God forbids, namely, that you must not needlessly put yourself in the occasion of sin.

For some persons, for many persons in your circumstances, to date a divorced man might be an occasion of sin. You are the only one who can decide whether or not there is any danger. But, sister, be careful. You say you passed up many chances. Don't forget that sometimes what is forbidden has a peculiar attraction of its own to our peculiarly weak human nature. And divorced men can be lonelier and more in need of companionship and can, therefore, appeal more to the sympathies of a woman than the bachelors you have turned down. The moment you begin feeling sorry for a divorced guy is the time you had better look for another escort.

Q. *I know everyone is automatically excommunicated for marrying a divorced person. However, please explain why a parish issues them collection envelopes, accepts donations and solicits such persons for workers, then refuses them entrance into the church for burial.*

A. You make too much of this excommunication. To begin with there might be some doubt about excommunication in this case. The general law of the Church has no such excommunication. It was the Third Council of Baltimore that imposed the penalty of excommunication on Catholics who attempt marriage after divorce. The law is all but forgotten, primarily, I think, because it has no real meaning today.

An excommunication automatically incurred does not cut one off from association with other Catholics; it does not keep one from attending mass or taking part in parish activities. It may keep one from sharing in indulgences and public prayers of the Church, but it does not cut one off from divine grace or limit God's actions in any way. For practical purposes all it means is that a person under such a penalty may not receive the sacraments. But this applies to anyone living in a state of sin, excommunicated or not. So the problem of the persons you have in mind is simply that they may not approach the sacraments until such time as they remove themselves from the conditions they are in.

A good pastor sympathizes with many of these couples who find themselves in a situation from which there is no easy out. Many of them have children whom they are rearing in the faith. However serious the mistake they made in entering a union that cannot be sanctioned by the Church, they find it impossible to separate without harm to themselves and to the children.

Pastors do encourage couples in such a situation to remain as faithful to the practice of their religion as they can, by attending mass and religious services with their children and taking an active part in parish life.

God has his own way of taking care of souls in this predicament. I recall several instances where the children of such unions received vocations to the religious life. And of the many persons I have known who remained faithful to the Church in spite of bad marriages, I cannot remember one that did not receive the sacraments before death.

Q. *Twenty-eight years ago my husband divorced me and married another woman because I couldn't have children, and she was pregnant by him. Two years after the divorce I married a widower with three children before a Presbyterian minister.*

I understand that people like us are recognized as fully members of the Church but living in mortal sin.

For three-and-a-half years we have been living as brother and sister, without sexual relations. My question is: May I go to confession and communion if I continue to live in this manner?

A. Yes, you may. Many couples have solved a similar problem in this fashion. I suggest you ask your pastor whether there are any formalities that need to be observed before you go to confession. In some dioceses permission of the bishop is required.

In the past these permissions were often given reluctantly. Perhaps with good reason. I remember the first time I sought such permission for an elderly couple. The chancellor, who incidentally did obtain the permission, told me of an experience the previous bishop had.

A pastor had talked the bishop into granting permission to a couple in their early forties to live together as brother and sister. "They're a great couple, bishop, bringing up a large family of splendid Catholic kids," the pastor argued.

A year later the bishop met the pastor and asked about how his remarkable couple was coming along. "Well, bishop," he replied, "I guess you could say they are still raising a splendid Catholic family. Last Sunday they brought in twins for baptism."

Please don't misunderstand me. I am not making light of your problem, but merely pointing out that what you are hoping to do is not possible for all. But it is possible for many advancing in years or suffering from illnesses.

It would surely be a work of mercy to inform such people of the possibility of returning to the sacraments. They need each other, and they need the grace of the sacraments. Tell them that there is a way to have both.

And now I want to say something else that I hope will not be misconstrued. You describe your situation as "living in mortal sin." According to textbook morality this would be true. But textbook morality is sometimes inadequate for judging the unique experiences of real, live human beings.

Living in mortal sin means remaining in a situation in which you deliberately choose to be turned away from God and prefer a creature to the Creator. Objectively speaking, judging the action apart from your own intentions and the reasons that motivated your decision, to attempt marriage when you were not free to marry would be a turning from God to a creature. Perhaps this is what you did, but then again perhaps you did not turn completely away.

You may have been so terrified by the thought of living the rest of your life alone or so overwhelmed by your maternal instinct to care for three motherless children that you honestly decided that what you wanted to do was good and not necessarily a turning from God. Neither you nor I nor any human is in a position to know for sure how God judged your decision. And you can take consolation from the realization that God is more merciful than moral theologians.

But granting, for the sake of further discussion, that you did sin grievously by marrying a second time, have you all these years lived in mortal sin? Once you became the almost indispensable mother of three children, were you free to leave? And presumably all through the years you have longed to return to the sacraments and to be right with God. Is it accurate to describe someone in such a situation as living in mortal sin? I don't think so.

Q. *I married a man who professed a belief in "free love," and for eight years he played the field, though married. I couldn't feel that this was a valid marriage. I divorced him. Two years after that I met a good Christian man, though not a Catholic, and two years later we were married by a Justice of the Peace. This man, as I do, believes that when two people are married they do indeed become one, forsaking all others. We have been married sixteen years, and I do feel that this contract is the valid one.*

I have talked with my pastor about a church annulment of the first marriage, but who can prove a party had intentions of doing or not doing any particular thing at the time the contract was entered into? What do I do? I can't give up the successful marriage I am now in and yet I want so much to receive the sacraments.

A. Present your case to your local Catholic marriage tribunal. It may be that the man's subsequent conduct can be used as evidence that he entered marriage without any intention of being faithful. This is, indeed, hard to prove.

You may be encouraged, therefore, to learn that your situation and that of thousands who suffer with you, has in recent years been given serious consideration by moral theologians and that some of these have decided there is a solution for you.

Our Church has long recognized that at times her laws can work hardships on certain individuals and so she admitted the possibility of settling a problem privately that could not be handled publicly by a church court. What was done in an ecclesiastical court or by a public decision of a bishop was considered done "in the external forum"; what was done privately without any public effect was considered done "in the internal forum." Hence, for example, a confessor or pastor might be allowed by the Sacred Penitentiary in Rome to absolve a person from an excommunication or impediment in the internal forum and give him the sacraments though publicly or in the external forum the action would have no legal effect – in other words, so far as the public was concerned the excommunication was not lifted.

With this as background, I quote from one of the leading and most influential moral theologians of our time, Father Bernard Haering, C.SS.R., who has this to say: "There are [marriage] cases in which there is no practical doubt that the first marriage was not made in heaven but because of special circumstances an external forum solution could not be obtained. The penitent is a sincere person; he knows for sure the facts that prove the invalidity of the first marriage; but in view of the complicated canonical procedure he is not able to give the kind of proofs that are required by many ecclesiastical tribunals. If the confessor or pastor or tribunal official feels sure this is the situation, there should be no delay for an internal forum solution. If the persons involved live in a second stable marriage, they should be assured that, in conscience, they can consider their marriage as valid before God. In order to avoid trouble, they should not mention this situation in further confessions."

If you read this carefully, you will see that this possibility does not apply to everyone who "feels" his first marriage was invalid, but only to those who "know for sure the facts that prove the invalidity of the first marriage." Here are some possibilities: 1) The first marriage seems to be certainly invalid for reasons recognized by Church courts but there is not sufficient proof available; 2) the first marriage seems to be certainly invalid for reasons recognized by Church courts but a final verdict from a Church court cannot be expected for several years; 3) the first marriage is regarded as certainly invalid for a reason which many theologians and Church lawyers acknowledge as sufficient but Church courts do not yet accept.

The problem has been thoroughly discussed in the 1970 issues of *The Clergy Review*, a highly respected monthly published by and for the Roman Catholic clergy of England. In this discussion three English theologians, Fathers James McManus, C.SS.R., Kevin T. Kelly and Henry Allard, S.C.J. and Father J. Boelaars, C.SS.R. of the Academia Alfonsiana in Rome,

have agreed in substance with an article by
Bernard Haering written for the *Jurist,* publication of the U.S. Canon Law Society. Father
Haering has also published his opinion in Vol-
ume 55 of the theological periodical *Concilium.*

All these theologians are careful to point out
that they do not think that what they recommend
will destroy the Church's position regarding
the indissolubility of marriage. Father Haering
says: "I have not recommended that a priest be
permitted to allow divorced people to remarry
or that he should be able to declare a second
marriage legally valid . . . . My concern is for
the credible proclamation of the divine mercy
for contrite sinners who in a legally and eccle-
siastically regrettable situation are prepared
to do the best they can and who sincerely seek
God's will." And Father Kelly: "It is simply
trying to maintain a balance between the respect
owed to the external forum for the sake of the
common good and the right and need of this individual Christian to share in the signs of
Christ's forgiveness and redeeming love."

What these theologians now publicly support
has for several years been put into practice in
some European countries, and here in this
country there are retreat masters and parish
mission preachers who have been asking use of
it.

Whether the priests where you live are will-
ing and able to consider this solution for you
depends upon local situations and your own attitude. In some places people might be shocked
and scandalized by such a solution. Much depends, also, upon the kind of marriage you are

now in and how well you have tried to remain faithful to the Church as far as you were able.

Q. *I am going with a man who has been waiting for more than a year for an annulment from the Church. He was married less than a year when he was drafted into the Army. While he was gone his wife took off with another man. When he came home, she was gone along with their furniture and money. My mother wants me to stop going with this man and she keeps telling me of cases she knows of where it is taking six or seven years to get an annulment. Is this true? Also, the man received a letter from the priest who is working on his annulment advising that he must go see a psychiatrist for a "professional opinion." Is this a usual procedure in annulments?*

A. Our Church courts have just been given a new set of directives from Rome that should help speed up the marriage cases. But what takes time in any marriage case is the hearing of witnesses. Sometimes it is difficult to locate them and still more difficult to get them to testify. Here is where the parties interested can help push the cases along.

The use of psychiatrists for professional opinion is becoming more common every day in ecclesiastical courts. Our judges are recognizing that there are sociopathic individuals who are capable of succeeding in their jobs but unable to commit themselves seriously to one person in marriage. Some courts are even looking into the possibility that there may be a

radical incapacity so deeply rooted in the per-
sonalities of a couple that it can be judged that
it was impossible for them to live together
from the beginning of the marriage.

Whether your man can obtain an annulment
it is impossible for me to say, but I can assure
you that it need not take several years to obtain
a decision, if he himself will help the court
reach the witnesses.

Q. *What happens when a Catholic couple after
a divorce wants to marry each other again? Can
they marry again in the Catholic Church?*

A. The Church wants them to come back together, but they can't remarry in the Church
because they are already considered by the
Church to be married. They must, however, be
married again civilly. This is what usually happens: The couple obtains a marriage license and
renews their vows before a priest who sends
notice of the marriage license to the authorities
issuing the license who record the second marriage. No church records are made of the second marriage for, according to the Church, the
couple remained married after the civil divorce.

AND NEW MEDICAL PROBLEMS?

Q. *Has the Catholic Church anything to say about what happened in a Stanford University laboratory recently, where life was created in a test tube? The great strides in genetic research indicate that man will soon be able to develop a super race of men – even a new type of men able to live many hundreds of years or with small bodies for space travel or large brains to multiply the Einsteins at will. Is it blasphemous for man to play God? Or are you forced to admit that now that man has the power to control his own evolution he has power over nature itself; the universe is his and he doesn't need God anymore?*

A. What the Catholic Church will ultimately say about this I do not know. But if you want the opinion of one speculating member of the Church, I shall be happy to oblige.

I am thrilled by what happened at Stanford and excited by the possibilities of improving the human race opened up by genetic research. I do not think that efforts to find the secret of life and produce it in a test tube are blasphemous, and I am convinced that the more control man has over his own biological evolution the more he will need God's revelation and help to keep him from producing monsters or slaves instead of super men.

It's God's secret of life that man seeks to discover. And when he produces the basic molecule of life, he does it with ingredients that God created. He is not prying into forbidden secrets when he tries to produce life and improve it. God's invitation to man to join him in the work of creation I believe to be part of revelation: "Let us make man in our image, after our likeness; and let him have dominion . . . over all the earth." (Genesis 1:26).

The genetic scientist in his research laboratory is reflecting the image of God as he seeks dominion over the earth; he is no threat to belief in God; but he could be an awful threat to belief in man.

Power over nature is power over man. The human race is approaching the moment when one generation will have the power to destroy the accumulated accomplishments of the millions of humans who preceded them and to determine the type of existence of the billions who may follow them. Who will decide what kind of man should be developed through genetic mutations? What is man, after all, and what should become of him? These are questions that may soon make God and his revelation seem relevant and meaningful for folks like you.

Q. *What is the Church's stand on the morality of heart transplants? We were taught that to mutilate the body in any way during life or after death is a sin. One might reply that much good for another is obtained this way. But isn't it a sin to use a bad means to obtain a good end?*

A. Yes. We are never permitted to use an evil means to achieve good. However, to transplant a heart from a dead body is not to mutilate that body; it is to use that body for something good.

Mutilation of the body implies defilement, a harmful maiming deliberately intended to render the body crippled or imperfect or to desecrate a corpse. That hardly applies to a surgical technique designed to save or prolong life. But there are legal, ethical and social questions surrounding the heart transplants that do not concern the technique itself. The American Medical Association recently asked for the greatest caution in approaching this vastly complex operation. There is widespread feeling that there has been an unseemly rush by surgeons to get into the headlines or the medical journals. Though the operation holds tremendous promise, the success rate to date is almost negligible. Much more study and research is needed.

There has been controversy, too, over the legal point of death and what proofs are needed for a legal determination of death. Recognized leaders in medicine, law and theology have suggested a moratorium on the operations until there is a thorough evaluation of those that have already taken place and until all legal doubts can be resolved.

Then there is the question of priorities. Who will benefit from this advancement? Only those who can afford it or those most valued in the human society? Is medicine justified in concentrating so much time, effort and resources on a single, innovative technique when millions around the world do not receive even the most basic medical care?

These are some of the prickly issues which

surround the heart transplants. This new medical knowledge is good, not evil nor morally objectionable. The widespread doubt and apprehension springs from a worry over whether society will learn to use the knowledge wisely and well.

SOCIAL JUSTICE

Q. *Why does the Catholic Church now empha-size so strongly love and equality for Negroes? When I was young they sat in the rear of the church and were not allowed in our school, which was a Catholic school. And why did God make many different races if all are to become one mixed race and what race would it be called?*

A. How about calling it the human race? And wasn't that school you went to misnamed? "Catholic" means all, universal.

You do raise embarrassing questions. Indeed, the Catholic and the other Christian churches have discovered rather late that their religion requires them to accept members of all races as brothers in one human family.

It is a fundamental theme of the Old Testament that sin destroyed the unity of mankind and divided men into hostile nations that scattered apart to develop into different races. This is graphically illustrated in the story of the tower of Babel. It is a fundamental theme of the New Testament that the Holy Spirit was sent to overcome the divisiveness of Babel by bringing all races and nations together into the one Church that understands and accepts all tongues. The gift of tongues at Pentecost was seen by the early writers of the Church as the reversal of the division symbolized by Babel.

The human mind is slow to comprehend the meaning of what God has made known in Christ. St. Paul, for instance, accepted without question that Christ was the new head of the human race and that in him all mankind was to be united into an extraordinary union in which there would be neither Jew nor Gentile, male nor female, but all would be one. And yet he accepted slavery as something normal and not in contradiction to the dignity and equality Christ brought to the human race. Saintly churchmen of the Middle Ages believed that it was good to torture men into professing faith in Christ.

Respect for the dignity of man, the basic equality of all men and their right to freedom are notions founded upon God's revelation to men in both the Old and New Testaments. It took the Christians of the West a long time to recognize these as obvious conclusions to be drawn from the creed they professed. And let us be honest. There are conclusions yet to be drawn that future generations will blame us for not seeing.

Q. *The club I belong to refused membership to a Negro. Should I resign or should I keep my membership and work to change the policy? My friends say a private club has a right to select its own membership and that it is ridiculous to talk about the rights of Negroes to belong to a private club where they are not wanted.*

A. A private club has a legal right to choose its own membership and, therefore, the right to exclude whomever it wishes. But what is legal is not always moral. Whether a private club has a moral right to exclude a Negro just because he is a Negro is another question.

A legal right is one established by civil law. A moral right is one based upon the principles and assumptions that support a people and their way of life. If we assume, as we do in Western democracies, that every citizen should have the opportunity to better himself and advance as far in society as his talents and energy permit him, then we are admitting the moral rights of the citizens to such an opportunity.

A private club may limit its membership to people of a certain religion, age, national origin, educationl or cultural background and financial abilities without in any way infringing upon the rights of others to advance themselves socially and financially. However, when in a nation, almost universally, country clubs, athletic and social clubs organized by the prominent and influential citizens exclude Negroes – even those who meet all cultural, educational and financial requirements for membership – then we must honestly admit that we as a nation are putting limits upon how far Negroes may advance and better themselves. So long as such a situation prevails, we are making it difficult for Negro parents and the educators of Negro youth to inspire them to better themselves. Every time a cultured, successful Negro business or professional man is turned down by the prominent citizens of a city for membership in their club, the influence of the balanced Negro leadership is weakened and the power of the black radicals is strengthened. What I am trying to say is that clubs of the prominent and influential have obligations to minority groups that no other private clubs have.

Now to get down to your own particular dilemma. I think that you should stay in the club, get more people who think the way you do to join it, become an active member, serve on committees and run for office; then one of these days you may be able to change the policy of the club. If all those who oppose discrimination against Negroes quit the private clubs the discrimination will go on forever.

Q. *What's gotten into our young priests and sisters? What a spectacle they are making with their demonstrations in church or open letters to the press denouncing bishops for not doing enough for the Negroes. Strange that the bishops denounced have actually been way out in front of other bishops in their efforts to help the poor. How come?*

A. I don't know – unless more is expected from these bishops because of their past records.

I feel sorry for bishops today who are social minded and keenly aware of the Church's obligation to the poor. They are overwhelmed at the moment by the impossibility of financing Catholic schools. They can't see where the money will come from to accomplish all the splendid schemes their young clergy concoct for saving the inner cities.

But I also sympathize with the young priests and sisters who are impatient with how little the Church is doing for the poor and especially for the Blacks in our big cities. Catholics live mostly in the cities. They are the largest and best organized group in all the major cities.

Who is in a better position to organize and lead movements to improve the living conditions and educational facilities in the inner cities than Catholics? What greater moral problem is there to solve than the neglect of the poor? To ignore this problem is to debilitate the faithful who are not taught that the needs of others must be as much their concern as their own. To ignore this problem is to refuse to eliminate the source of countless other moral evils among those who must live in the slums.

Why have we held back so long? What are we afraid of? We never lack courage or manpower when it comes to organizing against indecent literature or the relaxation of an abortion law. We have never worried much over what neighbors thought about our getting involved in such activities.

These are some of the questions that bother young priests and sisters. To them the financial dilemma is a problem of priorities. Which is more important today, keeping our schools open or lifting up the poor? They opt for bringing the Gospel to the poor. I am not about to be in a hurry to say they are wrong.

FAITH AND INTER-FAITH PROBLEMS

Q. *Four years ago, a very close Catholic friend married outside the Church. I completely disowned her for it – in fact I haven't seen her since. It bothers me. Did I do wrong?*

I was taught that a Catholic was not to attend such a wedding and not to associate with the person, thereby showing disapproval. Was I uncharitable? Should I have continued our friendship as if nothing happened?

A. Deep down inside you, aren't you convinced that what was taught you was bad advice that led to uncharitableness? Maybe it was best not to attend the wedding, but did you have to desert your friend? What have you gained by showing disapproval in this manner? If many others of her Catholic friends treated her this way, the girl is probably embittered.

This is not the way Christ treated sinners. Today He wants to live in us, love others through us. With this in mind, go find the friend you left in need.

Q. *In this ecumenical age and with so many modern changes in the Church, what may parents do when a Catholic daughter plans to marry in a Protestant church? Would her parents and relatives be allowed to attend the ceremony? Could they attend a reception in their honor? Could the parents send out wedding invitations or marriage announcements? She sincerely believes in this religion.*

A. It is not possible to give a yes or no answer to your question. The parents, who know their child best, must make the decision. All I can do is give some guidelines to help them decide.

If the parents are convinced that their daughter is truly sincere in joining the Protestant church (and the longer this happened before the marriage the stronger the presumption would be) then they might conclude that she is doing no evil by marrying in the church of her choice. In this case they might decide to cooperate completely with the marriage.

If the parents fear that the daughter has changed churches just to get her man, then they must ask themselves: "How can her faith best be saved?" Will their refusal to have anything to do with the wedding shock the daughter into realizing what she is doing or alienate her from the faith and the family forever?

In any case of this kind there is the problem of scandal that must be weighed. Is there danger of giving scandal by seeming to condone the sinful action of one's child by cooperating in a marriage outside the Church? In these days of greater independence of children and loss of parental control, Catholic friends and relatives will ordinarily understand and sympathize with the parents in their dilemma. And it is quite possible that more scandal might be given to Protestants by what could appear to be a lack of love and interest in their child were the parents to avoid the wedding.

There is no ready-made answer to this very common problem. The old prohibition against attending marriages of Catholics outside the Church no longer is effective in applying social pressure to keep the young in line - if it ever was. Today when in doubt as to what to do in these situations, it seems to me better to choose the course that will keep parents, friends and relatives close to the one who "marries outside the church."

Q. *My niece was born and raised Catholic by parents who, during her teen years, abandoned their Catholic faith and joined the Episcopal Church. (They had been away from the sacraments almost since her birth due to their practice of birth control.) As a member of that congregation, my niece married in that church and my aunt was of the opinion that I would not be wrong to attend the wedding since my niece had long since renounced her Catholic religion. Now, granted she has committed a mortal sin by abandoning her faith, was she excommunicated as of that decision? Or when she married in the Episcopalian Church? Or could she simply, if she were of that mind, go to confession and return to the Catholic church and sacraments?*

A. I don't grant that she committed a sin at all. From the description you give of them, her parents did not help her understand or practice her Catholic religion. It is most doubtful that she had real commitment as a Catholic and may have decided she had an obligation to join her parents in the Episcopal Church.

Therefore, I agree with your aunt that it would be all right to attend her wedding. Though

there was no question of a formal excommunication on the part of the Catholic Church, your
niece cut herself off from communion with our
Church by joining the Episcopalians. If she de-
cides to come back to the Catholic Church she
would be obliged to make a profession of faith
and go to confession. She would also have to
renew her marriage vows according to the
Catholic form, for strange as it may seem in
this case, any one baptized in the Catholic
Church with some upbringing in the Church remains obliged to the Catholic form of marriage.
This is something that needs to be changed.

Q. *Would you please settle an argument for
me? I maintain that it is wrong to have a wedding shower or attend one where the Catholic
has married out of the Church since it shows
approval of their sin. Others say there is nothing wrong with doing it. I was outnumbered by
about 10 to 1 and am anxious to be corrected if
need be. I know many changes have been made
in the Church. What is the rule on this now?*

A. I don't think in this instance it is so much
a case of change in the Church as change in the
society in which we live. Attendance at a wedding shower or giving a gift does not today mean
approval of the marriage. You might very much
disapprove of the fact your friend was marrying
a drunkard or a lout and still attend a shower
or even organize one for her without in any way
approving her choice of husband.
There never was a Church rule covering the

situation you describe except the general principle that one is forbidden to co-operate in the sin of another. But giving a gift or attending a shower is a most remote co-operation, and if what I said above is valid might not be even remote co-operation.

Q. *My son married a Methodist. Is it my obligation to see that they have Catholic items in their home, like holy water, sick call sets, etc.? Is it my duty to tell her about the Lenten observances?*

A. It most emphatically is not. Your son is on his own now. Unless your daughter-in-law asks for advice or suggestions on religious practices, you can best contribute to the harmony of the young couple by keeping mum on religion. Give witness to your religion by the loving generosity and kindness you show to your daughter-in-law.

Q. *My husband is not Catholic, but signed the necessary papers so we were able to be married by a priest. Now that we have children he refuses to bring them up in the Catholic faith. Our first child he reluctantly allowed to be baptized; but in the case of the second, he flatly refused. I had it done without his knowledge. He will not let me take them to church. He threatens to leave me if I bring them up Catholic. Where does my obligation lie: with my husband or with my children?*

A. There is no either/or answer to this one.

Your children need a father; so your obligation to them includes an obligation to keep your family together if at all possible.

There is no entirely satisfactory answer to the problem of the religious upbringing of children in a mixed marriage in which both husband and wife have strong religious convictions. If the children are brought up in the wife's faith, the husband's religious sensibilities will be offended. If they are reared in the husband's faith, the wife will be forced to live with a troubled conscience. If they are allowed to grow up without any connection with a church, both partners will feel that they are shirking a very important duty.

Although many mixed marriages have succeeded because of much good will and self-sacrifice on the part of both partners, there is a very real risk in this kind of marriage that the whole tragic situation of a divided Christianity will be transferred into the home and especially into the children of that home. The religious dilemma is particularly agonizing in the case of a person like yourself who is forced to choose between the religious education of his or her children and a broken home.

In your case it would seem from what you say that your husband allows you to attend church. If so, you are luckier than some in your circumstances. Keep your family together. Live as good a Christian life as possible and pray that your example will spark a desire in the children to accept the Church freely when they are able to make the choice for themselves.

If the joy of your own faith shines through and

makes you a loving wife and mother, you may one day convince your husband and your children that your Church can be the source of unity and love.

Q. *My son married a non-Catholic. She promised to raise the children in the Catholic Church. Now she refuses to let the children be Catholic. My son knew from the beginning that she had no intention of keeping the promises. Now I wonder whether he can receive the sacraments.*

A. Granted that your son did wrong when he entered into the marriage knowing that his wife would not live up to her promises to raise the children Catholic, what are his feelings now? Is he sorry for what he did? Does he want to receive the sacraments? Is he determined by the example of his own religious convictions to win his children to the faith?

If yes to all these questions, then he is properly disposed to receive the sacraments – even though his wife will not let the children be raised as Catholics.

Q. *I have reared two children alone for ten years. They are now 17 and 19 years old. I have reared them as Catholics, and I attended mass with them until three years ago when one and then the other told me they no longer believed in God and they refused to go to church. I have tried every way possible to persuade them otherwise, but without success. What can I do to relieve my own mind?*

Q. *This morning my 18-year-old daughter refused to attend mass with all of us. She said that she "got nothing out of it." She is a girl with a good religious background and high moral standards. What can we do to get her to go back to church without her threatening to leave home?*

A. The youngsters are telling us old-timers something. If we don't get the message, then the future of the Church would seem to be bleak. There is no future for the Church without the young, for they are the future.

But Christ has promised that his Church will always have a future. What then should be our attitude? Even though the ultimate future of the Church is assured by Christ's promise, the immediate future is something else again. And the immediate future is our children. What will become of them? Will most of them lose the faith and only a remnant be left? God alone knows.

This is an evasive answer to give parents who are worried about the eternal happiness of their flesh and blood. What do they do when their boy or girl loses interest in religion or, worse yet, leaves the Church?

First of all, surely they should remember that God loves those children more than they do. In their prayers for their children they will have to admit this to God.

Secondly, they might humbly look at themselves and try to discover whether there is anything in their attitude toward the Church that soured the children on religion. This can be an excessively critical attitude toward the clergy and religious or the opposite, an obsequious infantile attitude toward them.

Then thirdly, they should honestly ask themselves whether their own faithfulness to religious practices is matched by love and generosity. If a teenager wants to leave home, there more than likely is something wrong in that home, no matter how religious the parents are. And if the very reason for wanting to leave is a dislike for the insistence upon religion in the home, then there is something the kids would call phoney in that religion.

Fourthly, parents must respect the right of their children to make their own religious commitment and not nag them about going to church. Many a young person, who might have returned to the Church after struggling through several years of doubt and have been better for the experience, has been embittered and turned forever against the Church by well-meaning but foolish parents who attempted to impose religion upon him.

There is only one way to win the young back to religion and that is by demonstrating to them that it works. If religion makes parents loving and lovable, the children will ordinarily want religion.

I used the word "ordinarily" with deliberation, for I am aware that occasionally near-perfect parents, successful with their other children, produce a black sheep.

Q. *My 21-year-old daughter was married last year to a very fine and good man of the Methodist religion. She was married by a priest in a Catholic chapel. She has now joined the Methodist church.*

We pleaded with her not to do this. The only answer we got was that her mind was made up and that it would be better if she and her husband were of the same religion.

What should we, as her parents, have done that we did not do? We sent her to Catholic schools, reared her to be a good Catholic, saw that she never missed mass on Sunday, taught her to pray before and after meals, at bedtime and when arising.

She lives a thousand miles from us and all we can do is write. In my last letter I wrote that I would not reject her for doing this, but I would pray that she would change her mind and return to the faith. I know there is nothing we can do but pray. But what happens to a soul like this after death? Can she serve God as a Methodist and still go to Heaven?

A. I'm sure Heaven has a large Methodist population, including, perhaps, some former Catholics. Only God can judge your daughter's motives, and only he will determine the status of her soul.

If she joined the Methodist church because of convenience rather than conviction, or because of pressure from her husband and his family, then, yes her defection is a grave offense. But if she acted in good conscience, sincerely convinced she can serve God best in her husband's church, and in that way be a better Christian wife and mother, she could well be doing the will of God for her.

I don't know what more you can do about the situation that you have not already done. You have made it clear to her that this change grieves and worries you and your wife. Continue to write to her and let her know that her decision to join the Methodist church does not mean an irreparable break with her family. Some day she may want to return to the faith. Then she will know she can count on your help and understanding.

We Catholics believe that in our Church we have the fullness of Christ's plan for humanity, and we find it hard to conceive that anyone born and reared a Catholic could ever turn to some other Christian church. What we fail to realize is that some who grow up in Catholic homes and attend Catholic schools somehow never experience the joy and enthusiasm that the faith properly understood and lived can bring. They find this sometimes in the lives of Protestant Christians who have made the most of their religious opportunities.

Many Protestants, totally committed to their religious beliefs, are free and open missionaries, they talk freely and enthusiastically about their faith among themselves and others. An association with such people can be a humbling experience for someone who considers himself a "good Catholic," but whose spirituality begins and ends with Sunday mass or a set of isolated religious practices which are performed out of context with the rest of his life.

We try to instill the good spiritual habits you mention and, with gentle but vigilant discipline, our children do learn. But they can be saying their bedtime prayers almost as mechanically and mindlessly as they brush their teeth.

I wish more Catholic families would talk about their faith, make it an intellectual exercise geared to the age and comprehension of the children. Too many parents, once children are in parochial school, assume they are learning and accepting everything that is needed. As the children grow older, prayer and faith become private, individual matters. Family devotions are rarely, if ever, practiced and religious discussion may not go beyond the stage of asking when was the last confession made.

Many Catholics feel shy, ill at ease or defensive when talking about their faith. So they are impressed, sometimes overwhelmed, by those who can speak naturally and enthusiastically about what they believe and why. This can be especially true in the closeness of marriage.

We need to do better by our children in this regard.

Q. *You confuse us all when you say that it may be the will of God that a Catholic joined her Protestant husband's church. We have the body of Christ, the sacrament of unity. We should be the magnets drawing others to Christ in the eucharist, not turning our backs on him. We should all shed a few tears when any Catholic leaves the Church.*

A. I agree. Evidently I did not make myself clear. I said that if the girl who left her church to become a Methodist acted in good conscience, she could well be doing the will of God for her. Obviously she could not look upon the Church as you and I do or retain our belief in the importance of the eucharist and leave in good conscience. What we have to face today, however, is that some of our chidren can go through Catholic schools or be brought up in a traditional Catholic home and decide, when the time comes for them to make their own personal commitment to God, that Catholicism is not for them. Their decision may be based upon a wrong understanding of what Catholicism is, but if they honestly do what they think they have to do, then they do well and they would sin by going against their conscience. I am not saying this happens often, but it can happen.

It may be objected that a child receives the gift of faith at baptism and that, therefore, he cannot lose the faith without sinning. The virtue or ability to believe is part of the gift of God given with baptism, true. But faith still depends upon hearing. The ability to believe helps only those who learn to know Christ and the Father he reveals.

The whole point of my previous answer was that in some Catholic homes and schools religion is taught and practiced in such a way that certain children cannot use their ability to believe because the objects of their belief are not properly presented to them. This, by the way, is precisely why today Catholic educators are experimenting with new text books and ways of teaching religion.

MINOR ECUMENICAL QUESTIONS

Q. *Is a minister allowed to go inside a Catholic cemetery if he wants to? I was told one time a minister had friends being buried in a Catholic cemetery and he was told he could not come in. Well, the day of the burial he wore a black overcoat and went through.*

A. Well, hats off to the minister. It must have taken a lot of courage to walk into such a ghetto.

In this post-Vatican II era, when Protestant ministers are permitted to take an active part in a wedding inside a Catholic church, surely it would be in order to invite one to join a priest at the graveside in offering prayers for the bystanders.

Q. *Would it be wrong for a priest to offer a funeral mass for a non-Catholic husband of a Catholic woman? He was always very active in parish life, frequently attended mass and took great interest in the parish school while his children attended it. He was always a generous financial supporter of the church, but he did not become a Catholic on his death bed. His widow asked the priest to conduct a funeral service for him in the mortuary, but the priest said, "Why not have a funeral mass for him in church?" The priest said to keep it quiet. Why? Was the priest breaking a law? Would such a funeral be permissable?*

A. I believe the priest acted correctly, but I want to discuss this problem thoroughly, for there is more to it than meets the eye.

The priest did break the law as interpreted prior to Vatican Council II. Moral theologians and canon lawyers used to teach that church law forbade the offering of a public mass for deceased non-Catholics; many of them taught that it was forbidden to offer even a private mass for such persons – meaning a mass in which only the celebrant knew what the special intention of the mass was.

The reasoning behind this seems incredible today. Here, for example, is the argument spun out in the 1952 edition of the Woywood-Smith *A Practical Commentary on the Code of Canon Law:* "Though we know that many Protestants are such merely because they happened to be born of Protestant parents (not from any spirit of opposition to the Catholic Church), still the fact remains that they are in the enemy camp just like aliens during a war. The Catholic Church cannot recognize them as members of the Church without sacrifice of principle. Wherefore it is unreasonable to request a priest to say mass for a deceased non-Catholic, whether a private person or an official of a state or nation."

Isn't that unbelievable? We have come a long way in a short time. Here is how Vatican Council II looks upon Woywood's "enemy": "The Church recognizes that in many ways she is linked with those who, being baptized, are honored with the name of Christian . . . . For men who believe in Christ and have been properly baptized are brought into a certain, though imperfect, communion with the Catholic Church . . . . All who have been justified by faith in Baptism are incorporated into Christ; they, therefore, have a right to be called Christians, and with good reason are accepted as brothers by the children of the Catholic Church."

This change of attitude and recognition that baptized separated brethren share, at least partially, with us in the Church of Christ requires a re-interpretation of many church laws that used to regulate our relations with Protestants. In fact, the instructions on ecumenical matters issued by the Vatican Secretariat for Promoting Christian Unity encourages us to do many things with and for other Christians which once were forbidden, such as joining together for formal worship on special occasions, acting as witnesses at Protestant church weddings, and even the giving of the sacraments of the Eucharist, Penance and Anointing of the Sick to Protestants in danger of death or in urgent need.

There is no one closer to the Catholic Church than the baptized Protestant married to a Catholic. This person shares with a Catholic the sacrament of marriage and helps create in the home a church in miniature.

With this in mind, let's now take a look at the situation you described. If the man were affiliated with another church or his immediate family, brothers and sisters, desired a Protestant ceremony, the honorable and charitable thing for the widow to do would be to assist his relatives in arranging a Protestant service. But if he were like so many in such a situation, no longer affiliated with any Protestant church and for all practical purposes identified with the Catholic Church, why shouldn't he be given a funeral mass? There is no canon law that specifically forbids this, merely a traditional interpretation based upon a theology outmoded by Vatican Council II and handed on from generation after generation of theologians and canonists who never dreamed that such a situation could exist. If, therefore, there are no diocesan laws forbidding it, I feel that a pastor could make the decision yours made. I wish our bishops would recommend this.

Q. *What part may be taken by non-Catholics in a Catholic wedding?*

A. Any part.

Q. *During the Church Unity Octave, Protestants, Catholics and Orthodox joined in prayers for unity. What were we all praying for? Were Catholics praying that Protestants see the light and recognize the Roman Catholic Church as the one true Church of Christ? Were Protestants praying that Catholics recognize the errors of their ways and give up the pope? Were the Orthodox praying that both Protestants and Catholics acknowledge that the Orthodox notion of the Church is the most acceptable for unity?*

What would be the honest way to pray for unity?

A. Why not pray for unity on God's terms?
There is a temptation for all of us in prayer

to persuade God to our own thinking. The Lord Jesus submitted himself to an experience that helps us understand what happens to us when we pray as we should. In that long prayer of his in the Garden of Gethsemane, Jesus was tempted to persuade the Father to reconsider the plan for saving men. "Abba, Father," he prayed, "all things are possible to thee: remove this cup from me; yet not what I will but what you will" (Mk. 14:36). And the Gospels report that he went back again and again praying the same words. In the end he wanted what the Father wanted. This is what prayer does for us if we persevere and pray as Jesus did with the willingness to submit.

We begin almost every prayer by wanting something that we think good and necessary. We ask for a cure from cancer; we think it necessary for those who depend upon us. We sincerely and trustfully ask for it. We may get it, but the chances are we won't. But something happens in our prayer, if we pray as did Jesus in the garden. God communicates to us; he speaks to us by changing us so that we end by wanting what he wants; we trust completely the God to whom we pray.

If our prayer for Church unity is to be fruitful, then it must change us. "Lord, make your Church one," must ultimately mean: "Lord, change me so that I can help bring about the unity of the Church."

"I know, Lord," we should pray, "you want the Church to be one. Help me to love and respect others who differ from me in faith so that they can find your love in me and I find it in them. Help me to accept the unity of the Church on your terms; even if this means a period of agony and turmoil for us Catholics; even if this means giving up some of our cherished ideas about what the Church should be and how I should pray; even if it means I must accept a pope as head of the Church . . . ."

Now this does not mean we begin to seek unity by giving up what we believe. If Catholics, Protestants and Orthodox gave up what we each believe essential just to get along with one another and create a unity, we might have a unity, but it wouldn't be Christian unity, there would be nothing but a watered-down Christianity left. Each Church best brings about unity by better understanding and living its own faith.

We Catholics afford a good example of what this means. The recent Vatican Council was a mighty effort to understand ourselves better and this led us to discover how much we had in common with Protestants and Orthodox and how much we could learn from both. The new look at ourselves helped us rediscover ancient teachings of the Church hidden from us in the smoke of the long battle of defense against the over-emphasis upon them by the Orthodox and Protestants, such as: the presence of Christ in the words of scripture as well as in the sacraments; the priesthood of the laity; the mysterious, spiritual unity of all Christians in a Church that is larger than the visible community; the idea that church authority must primarily be a service to others, not a power over them; the sharing of the bishops in the authority of the whole Church.

The better understanding of ourselves that Vatican Council II led us to has given us a fresh approach to Church unity. The Council freed us from the illusion that uniformity is necessary for unity and presented a formula for a union of churches based upon variety and respect for freedom in these words: "All in the Church must preserve unity in essentials. But let all according to the gifts they have received enjoy a proper freedom, in their various forms of spiritual life and discipline, in their different liturgical rites, and even in their theological elaborations of revealed truth."

We Catholics are no longer praying for a return of Protestants and Orthodox to the Roman Catholic Church; we are praying that all the good that the Spirit of Christ has produced through the Roman Catholic Church, the Protestant and Orthodox Churches will help complete the Church of Christ and bring it to a fullness and a beauty and a miraculous unity with diversity that will make it the proof that Christ is from the Father and that the Father loves us all even as he loves his own divine son. This was the prayer of Christ at the Last Supper (John 17). What that unity will be like when it comes is God's secret. Our prayer will be honest and Catholic so long as we pray for the unity God wants.

Q. *When attending the funeral of a non-Catholic friend, the hymn books are sometimes passed out for congregational singing. Are we Catholics permitted to enter into the singing of these hymns?*

A. Yes. In the directions issued May 14, 1967, the Secretariat for Promoting Christian Unity gave this advice: "Catholics may be allowed to attend occasionally the liturgical services of other brethren if they have reasonable ground, e.g., arising out of a public office or function, blood relationship or friendship, desire to be better informed, an ecumenical gathering, etc. In these cases . . . there is nothing against Catholics taking some part in the common responses, hymns and actions of the community of which they are guests – so long as they are not at variance with Catholic faith."

It is altogether unlikely that you would be asked to sing a hymn at variance with the Catholic faith. The fact of the matter is, in my opinion, that most Protestant hymns are far more Catholic than the sentimental, meaningless conglomeration of worn out adjectives that we oldsters learned as Catholic hymns in our youth and now find missing in our new hymnals.

PAROCHIAL AND SMALL PROBLEMS

Q. *I long for an old-time sermon about Christian family life. The young priests these days are doing their best to make us neglect our family obligations. I was taught that charity begins at home. Is that too old fashioned?*

A. No, but be sure you understand the meaning of the phrase. There are priorities in love. We must love God first of all. A man must love his wife and children and place them before any obligations to neighbors or starving children in India. But how do we know our love is true, is not selfish? Some people who think they love God love only themselves and God for what he can do for them. Some parents who think they are devoted to their children are fundamentally selfish; they are possessive; they are seeking their own gratification in their children without realizing it.

Love is expansive, not restrictive. The more you truly love a person, the more you want to extend that love to include many others. So the test of love is how expansive it is. If the love of God is true, it impels us to love our fellow man. If a man truly loves his family, he will be a loving man; he will be interested in his neighbors, in the poor of his city, in the needy of the whole world. If he is not, because his family is absorbing all his time, then he had better have doubts about the validity of his love for his family.

Suburban man is the great offender here. He thinks of himself as a great family man, but so frequently he has no other interest than his family. He is not even aware of the horrible conditions of the inner city, let alone the poverty of South Americans. Perhaps this is the problem the young priests are talking to. They may be doing more for the Christian family than you realize.

Q. *Our pastor says it is against the Canon Law of the Church for women to go bareheaded in church. He says regardless of what newspapers and magazines have printed, the Pope did not change Canon Law. What is the ruling? Has there been any change?*

A. Your pastor is right. The Pope did not change the canon law requiring head covering for women at Mass. The news services misled us. But Church laws can cease to bind without any direct action by the Pope. As customs and circumstances change, laws made for past situations come to have no meaning. The same Canon Law (1262) which requires women to wear hats in church also encourages the separation of men and women in church. Prior to the publication of the code of canon law in 1918, this was a church law that had been almost universally disregarded for centuries. It appears to me that what happened to the custom of seating men and women on different sides of the aisles is in our time happening to the custom of wearing hats.

There is another observation I should make.

The law requiring women to cover their heads orders men to uncover their heads in church or outside church during religious ceremonies. It makes exception, however, for places where it is customary for men to keep heads covered in religious ceremonies. The law had in mind the customs of some oriental nations. Well, it seems to me that in the world we live in, the custom requiring women to appear in public with head covered no longer prevails; the contrary custom is in force. It would seem fair to conclude that the exception applied to men in China, should apply to women in Western civilization today.

Does it really make any difference? Pastors who insist upon imposing a law that no longer has any meaning or significance are waging a hopeless battle.

Q. *Would you please tell me if it is a sin to sew on Sunday or Holy Days?*

A. Not today. The Church law forbidding servile work on Sundays and holy days had a double purpose: to assure that servants and slaves had time off once a week to pray and worship God and to afford them one day of physical rest out of seven. Old moral books used to distinguish between sewing that was labor and sewing that was art. It was forbidden for the servants to darn socks or make dresses on Sunday, but the lady of the manor was permitted to crochet or embroider. This was not discrimination but simply protection for the servants. What the lady of the manor did was not considered work but recreation or diversion.

All this seems unrealistic today when ordinary people live better than most kings and queens did back in the Middle Ages. In other words, you are pretty much in the position of the lady of the manor. Sewing for you is not servile work - even darning socks would be something you do with your hands instead of holding a cigarette while watching TV.

Q. *Is it wrong to take horoscopes seriously? Has the Church any official teaching on astrology and horoscopes? Someone told me that in the past, popes considered astrology a science and made decisions according to the stars. Is this true?*

A. Initially the Christian Church opposed astrology which pervaded all the ancient cultures, the Greek and Roman in particular, and in the early days of Christianity had become an integral part of the pagan religions.

St. Paul in Galatians (4:9-11) is probably inveighing against pagan astrology when he writes: "Once you were ignorant of God and enslaved to 'gods' who are not really gods at all; but now that you have come to acknowledge God - or rather, now that God has acknowledged you - how can you want to go back to elemental things like these that can do nothing and give nothing and be their slaves? You and your special days and months and seasons and years! You make me feel I have wasted my time with you."

However, astrology was too much a part of

everyday life to be easily eradicated. It flourished among the Arabs, who spread it in Spain and Sicily and in the rest of Christendom through contacts made during the Crusades. So common was astrology in the Middle Ages that even St. Thomas Aquinas attributed sex and general character, in humans, to the stars. By the time of the Renaissance, astrology had become an accepted science.

Pope Julius II used astrology to set the day of his coronation and Paul III to determine the proper hour for every consistory. The leading astronomers, like Copernicus, Galileo and Kepler, were usually astrologers also. My source for this information is *The New Catholic Encyclopedia.*

The telescope did eventually explode most of the involved theories of ancient astrology. Nevertheless, there is a growing interest in horoscopes today, and astrology has taken on a certain respectability because scientists do seriously study the effects the heavenly bodies have upon the earth.

The claims of popular astrologers in the horoscopes found in newspapers and magazines are preposterous. They are based upon theories elaborated by ancient peoples almost totally ignorant of the knowledge we now have of the universe. To take these horoscopes seriously is not so much sinful as stupid.

Q. *At the time I became a convert it was stressed that one owed a supreme duty to his own parish, the parish in which he resided. Now*

I find parishioners do not seem to regard it as a serious duty to attend their own parish church. Rather they attend where they "like the priests" or "enjoy the homily" or "feel their efforts are appreciated." Ideally, I suppose, one should attend the church where one is happiest, without decreasing one's normal contribution to one's own parish, but we are not all rich enough to do this. Is there any church law on this?

A. No matter how I answer this one I am going to get into trouble. There is an obligation to give one's fair share to support the Church. This means the universal Church with its missionary activities, the diocese and the parish to which one belongs. But what parish? There's the rub.

I am pastor of a city parish. I know there are people living within the parish boundaries who don't like the way we sing and receive Communion standing. They prefer what they call a more "traditional" Mass and parish. So they go to one of the neighboring parishes. On the other hand, there are some living within the boundaries of other parishes who prefer our way of doing things. So they ask to join our parish. Why quibble about it? Why should such people be obliged to belong to a parish where they are not happy or at home? The people of God should be free. Thank God they are going somewhere to mass these days. That's the way I look at it, and I think most city pastors would agree. This may be stretching Canon Law a bit; but laws are interpreted by customs, and church-going customs are changing these days.